SERENDIPITOUS
LIFE EXPERIENCES

Rickey Williams II

Library of Congress Cataloging-in-Publication Data

www.rwilliamsii.com
Email info@rwilliamsii.com to book Rickey Williams II for your speaking engagement
Social Media: @r.williamsii

Rickey Williams II,
Serendipitous Life Experiences
Edited by: Patrick Bennett
Cover Design and Formatting by Cassy Roop of Pink Ink Designs
Published by: R. Williams & Associate, LLC: P.O. Box 346 Marietta, GA 30061

LCCN: 2016902525
ISBN: 978-0692643440

DEDICATION

You gave me my foundation and thank you for it. When I say you, I'm talking about:

My Grandmothers – I know you two can see what God is allowing me to accomplish. Thanks for talking with him in those moments when I didn't deserve his blessing.

Mom & Dad – No matter what you support me. You'll never understand how much that means to me.

Ashley – Like a second mom even though you're my sister. I could always depend on you.

Schwanna – My sister you always told me to follow my passion and I thank you.

To the rest of my family and friends, I could have never accomplished anything without what you all have deposited into my life.

I LOVE YOU ALL.

CONTENTS

INTRODUCTION

ISOLATION. HEARTACHE. UNEXPECTED EVENTS. All terms that society would deem non-beneficial in my experience bank. Instead I decided to classify them as "Serendipitous". Granted, these events stimulated emotions stereotypically associated with melancholy but my perspective forced me past that position. In my mind what seemed to be working against me was actually working in my favor. Being the whole point of why they are Serendipitous Life Experiences.

Also When I pondered over my life I was reminded had I never went through what I went through I wouldn't be able to convey the understanding of the outcome. What am I saying? Not only do we go through situations for ourselves but others as well. A mentor of mine once told me that observations are just as good of a teacher as experiences because there are a lot of circumstances you'll observe that you'll never want to experience. My experiences can serve as observations for you.

I'm not revealing my business, instead I'm telling you how to make it through from what I went through. Apply it to your own circumstance hopefully as prevention measures first but if need be reactive too. I make no claims to be an expert on the subjects I speak on; only on my experiences. In order for me to be an expert on my experiences, I had to experience it. I know that you'll obtain a great lesson from your observations of my experiences. Enter into my Serendipitous Life Experiences.

SILENT LUNCH

MY MOTHER TAUGHT SCHOOL FOR over three decades, retired, and went back to teaching. Now that's passion and purpose! During those three decades I had the honor of her being my six grade science teacher. Now let me explain what that meant. I had to work even harder than the other students and behave better than they did. This was all done to keep anyone from assuming that I was given a special privilege. Although I wanted to appease my mother, I wanted so badly to fit in. We all know that acceptance by your peers at young ages like 11 and 12 attributes greatly to a child's confidence. It didn't matter how cool or how down I thought I was, I couldn't have the best of both worlds. Knowing that the teacher was my mother made the majority of the "popular" kids shun me. Without open defiance I knew I could never at least be on the waiting list to be accepted.

So the day finally came where my need for acceptance outweighed the desire to do right. I took it upon myself to act out which was the worse idea. For most students my level of acting out would've never reached their parents because it wasn't overboard. It was an issue that a simple teacher implemented disciplinary action would handle. By this time it should be apparent that I didn't stop to think that I'd have to deal with the consequences at school and then at home! Mom is the teacher and the teacher is mom. My goodness!

Anyhow the punishment from "Mrs. Williams" was silent lunch. If there was anything more irritating than silent lunch in middle school please let me know. Lunch was your time to converse with your friends and rest your mind from the labors of the schoolwork. Here I am off from the rest of the students and as if that wasn't enough I wasn't allowed to talk. My mother didn't play games with her students, when you were on silent lunch you weren't allowed to laugh or chuckle. Well you're probably saying you weren't surrounded by any others so not talking and laughing shouldn't have been an issue. Being restricted from my natural form of communication was difficult. You had to actively think to bridle your speech.

When I look back at this story I find so many benefits to a situation that appeared to serve as a punishment. Serendipitous? Yes!

Just like silent lunch the world can be very much the same. You are surrounded by so many people yet alone. For many the perspective in this matter would be that silent lunch was a punishment, but it was actually meant for me to work on myself. I was given time to be alone and think. That's the point many of us miss when we find ourselves isolated from the world. We spend more time crying than seeking. Life will place us in periods of isolation. In these periods it's up to us to use time wisely. In my life I have experienced periods of isolation that seemed over bearing. Here are some points that I've learned during these times:

LESSONS LEARNED:

-   This is the time for you to evaluate yourself. Take a good look at you in mirror. Accept responsibility for you being there. I was on silent lunch because I wanted to be like everyone else but while there I realized that I'm not the same as everyone else. I had a higher calling. Because of whose child I was more was expected out of me. For all reading this that believe in God like I do let that previous sentence marinate in your mind for a moment. I found my worth during my period of isolation.

-   Discover what it is that you want out of life. Develop ideas and strategies for achieving the goal(s).

- What do you do when no one is watching? Do you operate as if you are being watched or do you slack off? Your answers to these questions give way to your integrity. How high is your integrity? During silent lunch eyes are not always on you. So do you remain silent or try to sneak some words out? Develop a strong integrity during your time of isolation. When you are able to do right when no one is looking it becomes second nature. Therefore when you are surrounded by others you don't have to think about your every action, you automatically do right.

- I found myself having more time because the usual distractions were isolated from me. (Last sentence was a gross change of perspective – "isolated from me" not "me isolated from them"). Now I'm able to enjoy my meal. Since they were isolated from me the time I spent conversing was now open. I could focus more on enjoying the meal. Isolation swimmingly granted me the opportunity to enjoy one of the basic necessities of life – food. Without nourishment how can you live? Your isolation provides you the opportunity to cherish the small things in life.

- It doesn't matter your relationship to life, you are never above its discipline. Regardless if you were born into privilege, you are not too high to get touched by life's isolation. This is my mother but here I was on silent lunch because she was exhibiting fairness in her judgement. Most importantly she knew that placing me by myself would help mold and shape me. Uncomfortable? Yes! Do I regret it? No.

- It is a period of observation. Look around and notice how people act from afar. It's amazing what you'll discover from just listening and watching. Afterwards I can guarantee that you'll be mindful who you allow to eat with you.

- Lunch was just a period like the classes of the day. What does that mean? Well, it had a starting time and an ending time. Your period of isolation is the same. Now I can't tell you how long the period is but what I can let you know is that it will come to an end.

To this day I'm not afraid to eat by myself. I've discovered that I have the ability to learn so much when I'm to myself. Embrace silent lunch!

MAN AWAKEN

THEY SAY CHILDREN EVENTUALLY move from doing as their parents say to as their parents do. I can recall many times my father and me taking rides together throughout the city where he would just impart knowledge upon me. This knowledge had a wide range of topics but overall he was preparing me for manhood. Not only did he tell me but he showed me how a man covers his family and interacts with his community. Growing up in that type of environment harbored maturity beyond my years. In the mist of these lessons I assumed manhood was synonymous with maturity. When I came to, I realized that maturity is just a crumb from the loaf of manhood.

It was a day in May 2008. Feeling great, I was getting ready to walk across the stage for high school graduation in a few days. This particular day I was supposed to be headed downtown to play the drums at a concert. I called this young lady that I had known for going on a year. We both had gotten to a point where we could no longer resist the calling of our lustful desires for each other. Thinking I'm being sly, I left the house early. I gave my parents some excuse about having to go get some extra equipment from my best friend's house. That way if they got downtown before me they wouldn't question my whereabouts. The young lady and I met up. Since this is not that type of book, I'll just say we fulfilled our desires for one another.

As the summer progressed the time drew closer and closer for me to go off to college. That first week of August I received a phone call. When I saw her name across the screen I got excited. Normally that meant another meeting, but this time the conversation was different. I could hear the tears fall in the silence that she exhibited once I answered. Immediately I asked what was wrong. She responded by telling me that she believed she was pregnant.

At that point in my life I had never experienced a heavier weight. The most important thing to me at that specific point was that she knew I wasn't going anywhere. The reason I made that remark was because she and I both were in relationships with other people. Yes, I was a cheater. Not all decisions I've made I'll say I'm proud of, but I can say they have aided in developing me into the "Man of Wisdom" I am today.

She went on to explain that her tears where not a result of her being upset that she could potentially be pregnant with my child but that this could keep me from going to college. While my lips uttered words of consolation to her, my heart was racing laps around the world. As that day went on I found myself going on one of those traditional rides with my dad. My silence became a dead giveaway that something was wrong. To me my silence was just me in deep thought. I'm thinking to myself will I be able to provide for her and this child? Go to college? This is not something that's expected from a child like me. My upbringing should have placed me so far from a situation like this. The thought process was broken soon as my dad started asking questions.

"Son what's going on? I know something is wrong."

"Nothing I'm fine," I responded.

How am I going to tell this man that my life is getting ready to take an abrupt change? What will he say? But then I remembered everything that he had previously said. At that exact moment the Man in me was Awaken. Everything that needed to deal with this situation was already within me. Over the years my father had been planting seeds within me with his many lessons. Now prior to this point I really thought I was a man, but I realized quickly that wasn't true at all. I had a level of maturity that exceeded many others my age. As for manhood I lacked greatly.

Questions that weighed me down earlier that day where no longer an issue to me. I never again asked myself what am I going to do but rather how am I going to make this work. Don't miss what I'm saying please don't. From watching my father and listening to the things he taught me I came to the realization that a man doesn't seek other choices from his responsibilities. Rather he seeks ways to get them accomplished.

Not going to college wasn't an option nor was not taking care of my potential child. On the road to developing my methods of accomplishment I started thinking not only about what my dad has said but the things he has done. His action of actively covering his family spoke louder than any words ever could have.

LESSONS LEARNED:

- For a brief moment I want to talk to the males. Being a man is never in the creation of a child but in the fathering of that child. Your life is no longer your own. Everything that you do should speak to the fact that you want your seed to germinate in better soil than you did. I didn't grow up poor nor in lack. Did I receive everything I wanted? No. Did I receive everything I needed? Yes. My parents created an environment conducive to the productive individual I am today. When this situation occurred I wanted to emulate that same environment but on steroids.

- Many times we waste a lot of time trying to figure out other choices when there is but one. Our time can be more effectively spent discovering ways to complete the task at hand. My first instinct was will I be able to. Then it shifted to how I will be able to. This drastic permutation in mindset stem from the understanding that the only option was to take care of her and the child and go to school. When I came to that conclusion all my brain power went to making a way not debating a way out.

- Who we need to evolve into sometimes has to be drawn out of us. You have to remember life doesn't care what lights the fire to move you, just long as the flame gets lite. I had everything I needed to be a man yet I wasn't one. Age didn't make me a man it was my mindset. Up to that point I didn't have an urgent reasoning to think "man" therefore I didn't exhibit those characteristics. Whether a situation manifest itself or not, the possibility can sometimes be just what we need to shift into another level.

In the end the young lady turned out not to be pregnant. Here's the thing, even though she wasn't pregnant, the resulting mindset from the possibility of her bearing my child remain after this fact was exposed. In life we experience pains that cause growth – growing pains. Thankfully the growth remains after the pain.

MAN AWAKEN (POEM)

The seeds had been planted
But had not manifested
Here came the rain
The potential growing pain
This resulted in germination
Followed by elevation
A man growing
But not grown
Surrounded by what appears to be shame and failure
It was actually serendipitous I tell you
Man was asleep
A situation emerged mirroring defeat
Man was awaken
Victory was taken

WENT TOO FAR
(INTERLUDE)

A BEAUTIFUL SATURDAY AFTERNOON in January 2009 I decided to take a drive. By this time I was entering into my second semester of my freshman year of college. While driving I happened to go farther then I intended to. Crossing the train tracks entering into the "other side of the tracks" I discovered a place that would prove to be greatly influential in my life.

With my love for funeral service I never miss a sign that identifies a funeral home. After a few seconds I came across a sign for a funeral home that sounded so familiar to me. I begin to think back to a conversation I had with a gentleman prior to going off to college. He had told me the funeral firm I needed to become a part of when I got to the area but initially I couldn't recall. So I gave this gentleman a call which confirmed what I thought to be true. The next day I put on my suit, got my resume, and went back to that funeral home. When I walked into the building it was so peaceful. The owner was not in at that moment but his brother instructed me to leave my contact information. With my contact information, I left the name of the gentleman who informed me about the firm. Before I walked out he stated that the owner would be in later that day. My intent was to definitely come back at the end of the day. When I went back at the end of the day the owner was present. I introduced myself and his first statement to me was I had been looking for you for six months. By the end of the week I was working for the firm. That day I didn't know that I met my mentor in funeral service.

LESSONS LEARNED:

-   When I initially got to college I would have loved to be working at a funeral home but I was in a new environment. Forgetting the name of the place I needed to go provided a necessary blockage for me to get acclimated to dealing with my schoolwork. We have to learn how to deal with the purpose before we can dabble in the passion. Had I went directly there I would have given 100% of my time and effort to that firm. Understanding proper balance, where time could be given and where time needed to be dedicated, was essential to my destiny. I needed school to aid in preparing me for the road ahead.

-   You have to go off the set path to encounter the true path. Knowing that I was going farther than I needed to go I could have easily turned around but I didn't. I found someone I was going to need for my journey.

What I really want you to take away from this event in my life is keep pushing. What's pass where you think you should stop may actually be exactly where you need to start. When you feel like turning around go a few more steps farther.

THE SEARCH

NO RELATIONSHIP IS UTOPIAN. Everyone has their flaws and their counterpart has to make a decision about what they're willing to accept. I met a young lady in my life that seemed perfect for marriage. Was she perfect? No. In her imperfections, the perfections that radiated from her made her perfect in my eyes. Cliché, I know but it takes experience to understand why it's true.

I can recall the first time I met her. She was one of the all-female panelists for a youth empowerment seminar I was speaking at through my organization. Now let me go ahead and say this was not a love at first sight happening. It would take a few more encounters before we actually engaged one another in a conversation. That day came after numerous crossing of one another's path on the college campus we were attending. One day I asked if she had a few minutes to talk. She took a few moments to converse with me afterwards exchanging numbers. Before I knew it we were talking frequently. The subjects were various mentally stimulating topics with a comedic relief attached to the exchange. When we would spend time together nothing else mattered to me. She was the only one that could make me tell the funeral home I'm not accessible at certain points in time. Here I am opting not to take part in something I never thought it was possible for me to live without, my passion, funeral service. However, for her it was worth breaking away from. To me we had what I felt in my mind and heart to be the ideal relationship prime for marriage. Did we have difficulties? Yes we did. It was nothing that kept me from attempting to fix the issue. A disagreement would bring out creativity in me I didn't know that I had. I had to let her know how much I wanted her in my life. There was something that radiated from inside of this woman that I had never encountered from any other woman I've dated at that point in time. When I sat back and observed her, it was her heart for people that took me by storm. To think that she would trust me with a heart like that was an indescribable feeling. After reading this many will say Rickey you are still in love with this woman. Well let me finish my story and you'll have the answer to that burning question in your mind.

I was a distance learning student completely enrolled in another school at this time. This particular school had a satellite campus in Savannah, GA. about 50 miles away from the campus we met at. When she and I met I was supposed to have moved to Atlanta, Georgia, which housed my school's primary campus. After establishing "a life" where I was, I decided not to move and utilize the Savannah campus. One day word came that the Savannah campus would start limiting classes to only graduate students. That meant for me to complete my bachelor degree on track I would have to move to Atlanta. Trying to get me to leave was like pulling teeth. I didn't want to leave the funeral firm I was at, the church I attended, and her…

Nonetheless I made my way to Atlanta. Not long after I moved we begin to experience issues. Initially I thought it was obviously because of the distance. To minimize this problem I would go back every second weekend of the month. The issues still remained. In my small mind of thinking I figured I needed to be around more. So I started traveling during the week. I went to class in the day, worked at the funeral home until 11 pm then I would get in the car drive three hours arrive at 2 am just to leave at 5 am to be back in Atlanta for my 8 am class. Now I know I know you say that's crazy. Six hours of driving for three hours. Those three hours of her presence was worth more to me than an entire eight hours of sleep.

After all my efforts the relationship still ended. Heartbroken was not even the word. I had never felt that type of hurt in my life. Honestly, it felt as though life had been taken from me. Now I no longer had this all access pass to her heart that I once had. Imagine being locked out of a place you called home for years. Where home is where your heart is. After the conclusion of the relationship I still wanted to be with her. I tried with every fiber of my being to transfer those burnt ashes of a relationship into a beautiful phoenix. I can recall one day talking with a close friend of mine who I consider a brother. He could feel the hurt I was experiencing every time I called him. He told me Rickey I can't understand why you are putting so much energy into a situation that's clearly over. I responded by saying you just don't understand what I've found in this woman and how she has changed me. He replied well if she is that important write out a list of all the things that draw you to her and another list of all the things that got you two to this point. But realize the list is not about quantity of items but the weight of those things. If after that you still feel you need to peruse her keep on my brother. But I need you to know I don't like this place you're in.

I made the two lists and decided to keep trying. After a year and a month of effort all communication ceased.

That was a lot to take in at once and I know there are numerous serendipitous events that occurred. I'm going to go through all of them. Ready? Let's go!

LESSONS LEARNED:

- First let's start with the disagreements her and I had when we were together. All relationships have disagreements. It's in these times that you discover how bad you want something to work. As I said previously I had to dig deep to find ways to place a smile on her face. She never required any extravagant gesture. A simple apology would have been enough for her. She didn't want to let go just as much as I didn't want to let go at that time in the relationship. For that reason alone I placed so much effort in pleasing her. Point: Our deep love for one another taught me how to appease a woman deeper than the superficial. All this occurred without crossing the threshold of the physical.

- There is an entire chapter dedicated to fully discussing the closing of the school in Savannah. So I'll only discuss that occurrence from the point of view of this story. It was difficult for me to accept the fact that there was a needed separation between her and me. In one of the earlier chapters, I talked about the benefits of silent lunch or the isolation period. You should have a firm understanding of why I say we needed separation but that would have never occurred had the school not closed. In this period of isolation I realized that the connection may have been strong but the relationship was weak. I never solely blamed her for everything that occurred. I took a good look at myself to see what I could improve on. The key thing to take away here is just because you were done wrong doesn't mean that you yourself are perfect. Instead of assuming the identity of the victim evaluate your short comings and move forward from that perspective.

- Now let's look at this situation overall from the point starting at the breakup. Have you ever eaten a sugar cane or a banana? If so then you understand the concept of peeling away the outer shell to get to the sought after part of the item. Just like that is what the break up served as. It was a hurtful ordeal but the title needed to be stripped away to get to the "heart" of the matter. The question to think about is does a title affect how much you are willing to do for a person or is it the connection? Even after the title was dropped I was willing to do things for her that many said I was foolish to do. An absence of a title showed me that I truly had a heart for her happiness. Let me place a pin here very quickly. If you are reading this and you think that I'm talking about her you are mistaken. This is about my discoveries about myself. About my heart. Remember this is still the isolation period. OK back to the topic at hand. Point is the true you is not defined by a title. Your true identity is revealed when you are relinquished of a title. The bare you is the real you. We can a have a deep conversation about what someone should and shouldn't do without proper titles. I want you to think about that job title you want. You have to exhibit those characteristics prior to receiving the title. In retrospect you have to be that person way before you are titled as that person. Who are you with no title?

- Recall my best friend telling me to write down the two lists. Once it became apparent to me that it was completely over I pulled out the list of things that I loved about her.

A LOVE THAT ENCOMPASSES THESE ATTRIBUTES:

- ✓ A heart for all
- ✓ Dependable

- ✓ Consoling
- ✓ Teaching
- ✓ Optimistic
- ✓ Forgiving
- ✓ My favorite: Unconditionally Loving

Just to name a few…

So conventional wisdom, wait I should say common thinking instead, had me searching for those characteristic in every other woman I met. In my quest I'd find women close to the list but none with the entire set of characteristics. Now I sat back, pondered, asked myself do I need to lower my preferences or would I be compromising my standards. Many times we confuse the two – **standards vs. preferences**. Immediately something said to me that what you are searching for is neither a standard nor a preference – it's an expectation of a promise. A promise? From who and when was this promise to me. The answer came to me saying:

"While you thought you were searching for her in another woman, you were simply yearning for the **God** that you encountered in her. God promised to be all those things you wrote down that you loved about her."

With my mind blown but with so much understanding at the same time, I got what I needed. In essence I was searching for someone that has always been with me. All my life growing up in church understanding God and how he cares about his people, it took a heartbreaking experiencing for me to truly search for God.

- When you truly find God you want to be in his presence as much as you can. Remember, I traveled a great deal and odd hours just to be in her presence. Now that you know what I was really seeking after you can understand the power of coming into contact with the presence of God. You'll never want to be apart. With all that's within you you'll do your best to remain with Him.

- Many times we go through life searching for people to fill voids when what we should actually be searching for is even higher than that. Now I don't know what higher power you answer to but mine is God – the Father, the Son, and the Holy Spirit. Please don't miss the message for the belief of the messenger. Message:

"Fill that void with a higher-being, a higher-calling, a high-purpose."

Now ask me again if I'm still in love with her and I'll tell you I wish her well in everything she does. No, I'm not in love with her any longer but she serendipitously helped advance my relationship with God. You can discover a perfect divinity in an imperfect humanity.

BLIND MAN'S LOVE (POEM)

When the blind man loves, let me tell you what he sees
For all that he loves has no connection with vanity
Love's silhouette is intellectual and spiritual
It's the vessel that represents the physical
He places his value in characteristics of the crew
Genuine attributes let him tell a vessel
he'll never see you're beautiful
For eternity he wants to be a part
Apart for 2 seconds breaks his heart
He had to leave the vessel, although
staying was once his plea
Immediately his eyes were open, yet he still could not see
Deep was the void accompanying a feeling of defeat
He discovered a love rendering him complete
Remembering as if it were yesterday
it was a member of the crew
Although end season for he and
the vessel eventually came due
He stood at the dock telling the love he now knew
This day I dropped a tear in the ocean blue
When I find it then will I cease loving you

SCHOOL CLOSING

PRIOR TO MY DEPARTURE FOR COLLEGE I had a timeline on how long I planned on staying in Statesboro. My plan was to stay for two years and then move to Atlanta to finish out my remaining three years of the Electrical Engineering program. Once I got acclimated to the environment and the people, the inclination to leave dwindled. I can recall one year I told my mentor I was going to go ahead a leave for Atlanta and soon as I walked out the door something said not yet. Listening to the voice I remained.

At the beginning of the 2011 – 2012 school term it was

announced the distance learning campus I was a part of would no longer offer the few classes I had left for graduation. This meant that I had to move to Atlanta to complete my course work. The last thing I wanted to do was leave Statesboro. I had no other option. Halfway into my last year in Statesboro the funeral firm I was working with experienced a great loss. My mentor's father passed away. He was instrumental in my mentor's life and the birth of the firm. My mentor informed me that a funeral firm out of Atlanta would be handling the funeral in conjunction with us.

They came down the morning of the service. I can remember the director from that firm asking me what was the plan for the day. We discussed what we would do and preceded forth to serve. When it was all said and done my mentor, the director from the Atlanta firm and I had a conversation. In the conversation the director from Atlanta said I need this man up there with me. Reason being stemmed from a closing speech that I gave at the gravesite. My mentor let him know that I would be moving up there in the coming August. He responded by telling me to come see him when I got there.

When I got home that evening, I looked up that specific firm online. Immediately I recognized the firm from many years ago. Going back to 2008, I was in a relationship with a young lady who lived in Atlanta, Ga. She knew of my passion for funeral service ironically being that's how we met. When I went to visit her, she took me to a funeral home. As soon as I laid eyes on the building and the vast fleet of cars in the parking lot, I said one day I'm going to work for this firm. That was part of the two year plan, although I didn't specifically recall the firm until that instance in 2011.

In May of 2012 a prominent funeral director in Savannah, Ga passed away. My mentor told me that I would be driving one of the limousines for the service. Limo number 17 was the placement of my vehicle. When we got to the funeral establishment in Savannah that morning, I saw a familiar color hearse (in my industry it's properly termed a flower car). Come to find out it was the same funeral firm out of Atlanta that I was taken to and who accompanied our firm on the service for my mentor's father. But this time it was the actual owner of that firm who was present. Known as the undertaker's undertaker it is the goal of many to work for his firm. During the service I got an opportunity to introduce myself to him. I told him I would be moving to Atlanta soon, just as his brother stated, when you get there come see me.

In August of 2012, I made the transition to Atlanta, Ga. As I was instructed I went to the firm. I met with the owner's brother and he allowed me to shadow him for some days. When he was unable for shadowing, I would just show up after class, greeting the families. When I initially saw the owner again he fail to remember exactly who I was. With the volume of people he had met only one time between Savannah and that point directly affected his lack of remembrance. Never did I allow that to stop me. For two weeks straight I showed up, greeted families and assisted wherever else I could. At the conclusion of that two weeks period the owner of the firm took notice of my persistence. His exact words were,

"Are you being taken care of son?"

I responded by,

"How so?"

"Are you getting paid?" He replied.

My answer was no. After hearing my answer he took me to the proper individuals he put in place to get me placed on the schedule and compensated. The only available positions they had were a few evening shifts. Ironically, that worked perfectly with my school schedule. About a month later the weekend night shift opened up. It was offered to me and I promptly accepted.

LESSONS LEARNED:

- I'm quite sure you've heard this before but timing is key to the success of any situation. Had I went to Atlanta when I wanted to I'd probably never gotten the opportunity to work with this firm. There are people who have been waiting years and applying multiple times to gain employment there.

- Don't forget about your declarations. Even if what you have called out to happen doesn't occur when you believe it should doesn't mean it'll never manifest. It takes preparation prior to manifestation. The road had to be aligned for the destination and you have to be prepared for the journey. An opportunity means nothing without proper preparation to meet it. It took four years for a declaration I made to come into existence. Why? During that four year period I was being molded for the declaration. In order for me to have the mental capacity to deal with the new environment, I had to be shaped.

- Our calling can require us to be on a larger stage than were we are used to being. Compared to Atlanta, Statesboro is obviously much smaller. This is NOT to say that you cannot be effective in a small area. So much was accomplished for me while I was there and even after I left. There are resources that I had been able to come into contact with since my move. I was introduced to various ways to serve in the industry that I love past the conventional and traditional.

- Passion is Persistence and persistence is valued. I love funeral service. It has been my passion since I was 17. It didn't take much effort for me to show up day after day without compensation. When the owner saw my persistence he also saw my passion. Whatever you are passionate about you should put forth as much effort as you can to operate in it. Take your mind away from the money and realize that it will come as long as you stay persistent.

BROKEN GLASS

IN LATE 2014 I MADE SOME statements for 2015 regarding what was next in my journey. No they weren't New Year's Resolutions for 2015. Instead they were verbal affirmations of declarations resulting from promises of God. I worked an every weekend night shift for the funeral home. Every Friday night, Saturday night and Sunday night from 11 pm to 9 am the next morning I had to be at the funeral home. It didn't bother me too much because I loved what I was doing but there was a deeper requirement of me brewing.

I would constantly tell my friend that was on the shift

with me that come 2015 I would be off the night shift. I knew that I would be more of an asset to the company during the day. Especially giving the fact that 2015 was the year I'd obtain my Funeral Director and Embalmer licenses. (Another declaration made and received.) When I first started saying I was going to switch shifts there was no room for me on the day shift. As the year progressed, word circulated that the firm would have a completely new location opening the first of the year. January 2015 came, the new funeral home was open, yet I was still working the night shift. A few more weekends came and went with me still saying I'm coming off night shift. On the last night of the last weekend I worked the night shift I came outside that morning to a broken window on my car. Out of all the years I had that shift I never encountered any issues like that. I knew at that instance the move had to be made. I let the HR department know of my request and the same week I was at the new location on the day shift.

LESSONS LEARNED:

-   When you become complacent in the current state, uncomfortably comes as a confirmation to fall into faith. Let's start at the beginning. Some people lack faith to move given what they see. This wasn't the problem I had but I feel I need to address it. It's easy to have faith when we can see the clear pathway. So is that really faith in the end? No. When you can't see the way but believe it's going to happen is true faith. First, ensure you have faith. Now what if I have faith. Ok here's what's next:

- Recognizing the confirmation to move. Once you have faith all you need is the go ahead to move forward. My confirmation was in my declaration but my comfortability restricted my maneuverability. The comfort in the position had to be disturbed to make me realize the confirmation to manifest the declaration to go to the day shift. The broken window made me so uncomfortable that I had no choice but to remove myself from that situation. It's not like a car being broken into wasn't common just a needed event to make me realize what I needed to do.

Have faith and recognize the confirmation.

PERIOD SPACE NEW SENTENCE:
CONCLUSION OF MOTIVATION

As I pondered on how to close out this book, I started flipping through a notebook where I randomly write out thoughts. I came across this speech that I wrote when I was getting back to my purpose in life. This speech was the second one that I wrote. As I read it, the meaning fit so well with the context of the book that I'd say the conclusion could have been the start of the book. I feel no other closing would be more befitting:

One day a sketch of your life will be written for all to read. For some this sketch will be destined for a large publication but for all it will be when you can no longer contribute anymore to the story. That time would be, as my late Uncle Andrew would say, when you've gone the last mile of the way. This sketch will contain the story of your birth, upbringing and most of the accolades you have accumulated. Whether you know it or not, every detail of your life will be written in this sketch. Now you may be saying Rickey how is that so. Unless this is an autobiography I don't think so. Even then there are some things that I would leave out. I'd even go as far as saying some of those details I would have taken to the grave with me. I get what you're saying I get it completely but if you don't mind let me educate you on the formation of a body of written work. See a body of written body of work is formed by building blocks called paragraphs, which consist of a group of sentences, each ending with some form of punctuation. Most commonly a period. I'm not sure about you but one of the first rules of grammar I was introduced to was between the ending of a sentence and the beginning of a new one there is a space…

Period, Space, New Sentence

For some reason that just resonant within me – period, space, new sentence. What I like to believe is that the sentence is merely the result of the space. I understand that nothing appears as though it occupies that place, but in all actuality, the space is what we know to have been our reality. Its emptiness is what results in its significance. The space is the ugly struggle of my story. For many years I was embarrassed about my space. For it contains the deepest and most intimate details of my life. Those moments I found myself isolated, thought about running from my issues, looking for a love I thought was lost. All these experiences filled my space. After each space emerged a new sentence. Something that I was proud to let the world know.

Embrace you space because it's what makes your story readable. You find resourcefulness in your space. You'll discover love in your space. You'll find patience in your space. Most importantly you'll find you in your space. Thank you for taking time to read about my space. I love you.

THE EXPERIENCE:

_____
_____
_____
_____
_____
_____

LESSONS GAINED:

_____
_____
_____
_____
_____
_____

THE EXPERIENCE:

_____

_____

_____

_____

_____

_____

LESSONS GAINED:

_____

_____

_____

_____

_____

_____

THE EXPERIENCE:

_____

_____

_____

_____

_____

_____

LESSONS GAINED:

_____

_____

_____

_____

_____

_____

"AND WE KNOW THAT ALL THINGS WORK TOGETHER FOR GOOD TO THEM THAT LOVE GOD, TO THEM WHO ARE THE CALLED ACCORDING TO HIS PURPOSE."

ROMANS 8:28

www.ingramcontent.com/pod-product-compliance
Lightning Source LLC
Chambersburg PA
CBHW060557100426
42742CB00013B/2598